On Being a Pastor's Wife and Loving It

By Dr. Paula Jacob-Fox

On Being a Pastor's Wife and Loving It.

ISBN 978-1-951113-05-6

Text copyright © 2019 by Dr. Paula Jacob-Fox

Cover design by DeAndra Hodge

Self-published in the United States with Kinly Publishing, LLC, Wyoming | www.kinlypublishing.com

Printed in 2019 in Dayton, Ohio

Table of Contents

Dedicated to:

Pastoral spouses around the world supporting the work of the Lord

Foreword

I know what you must be thinking. Is there something not to love about being a pastor's wife? In today's world, since approximately 10% of American congregants have a female pastor, the more appropriate question is, what's not to love about being a pastor's spouse? After all, the work of a pastor is among the most important in the world. These men and women are called to preach the Gospel of Jesus Christ to the world, win souls for Christ and nurture these souls through many important events in their lives. They are also called to be administrators of churches, institutions of higher learning and even large conferences. They represent the Christian community to world leaders and can be a voice for the powerless and the least amongst us. The role of a pastor is certainly a very noble and respected profession. So why would the spouse of a pastor not love his or her role? Why would they need encouragement to love what they do?

In this book, we will explore some of the challenges of supporting pastors, mostly from the perspective of a pastor's wife. We will also discuss ways to navigate the challenges associated with these roles, and learn how one can enjoy the process of being the support behind the scenes, the wind beneath the wings and the co-pilot of a pastor.

If you are a pastor's wife or spouse and you were either gifted this book, or decided to gift it to yourself, congratulations on choosing to empower yourself with the words that follow. I know what you've been told – You should not complain, or let your challenges be known. We are trained to wear the mask of perfection. We are told to just get on our knees and pray; don't dare publicly share our personal struggles. We are made to believe that we must fit the box of expectations set for us by others. Well, this book was designed to give you permission to be yourself, to express your frustrations and to know without a doubt that you are not alone in the challenges you face. Research has shown that despite the fact that pastors' wives generally love serving the church and being involved in ministry, there are some common challenges many of them face. Studies done by Lifeway Research found that of 720 pastoral spouses, 59% agreed that congregational demands interfere with their family's free time. Further, 69% of this population said they had few people they could confide in, while 68% worried about having enough money for retirement. Among these pastoral spouses 49% stated that if they were to be honest at church about their prayer needs, they would just become gossip, while 79% indicated that their congregation expected their family to be a *model family*.

As a pastor's wife, you are his chief caregiver, the one he comes home to when everyone else leaves. You devote yourself to caring for him, your children, and members of your church. Yet, it is also important to love and care for yourself. You have to fight for your marriage, your family and your health. It is important to preserve your individuality and nurture yourself spiritually. Unfortunately, the enemy knows how to push your buttons. He knows how to let discouragement and dissention creep into any family, but particularly into the pastor's family. He knows how to attack your marriage, to aggravate your children and to upset your sense of peace. He knows that if he can weaken the pastor's family, he can discourage entire congregations and undermine the work of the Lord.

This book is about how you can take back what appears to be taken from you. It's about loving your spouse, caring for your marriage and your family despite many challenges and spiritual attacks. It's about caring for your health and that of your family, despite leading busy lives. You see, loving the Lord and serving the church does not mean you have to abandon your needs. It does not mean you have to sacrifice your relationship with your spouse in order for God's work to succeed. It does not mean your children have to tolerate having parents who are always too busy caring for the families of others, that they neglect to care for their own.

In this book readers will learn about how you can survive being married to a pastor, while keeping your sanity, your marriage, your family and faith in the Lord intact. Anecdotal stories are shared for emphasis and to clarify the topic of discussion. Though based on real characters, the names have been changed to protect the identity of the true characters. I invite you to put your feet up, close the door, and read to find out how you can be married to the pastor and still be happy, healthy and blessed.

Chapter 1:

Married to the Man whose Work Never Ends

Let's begin with a personal story. I will tell you about a lady named Elizabeth. Let's call her Liz for short:

Liz is 40 years old and has been married to her pastor husband for over 15 years. They have 2 children: A boy who is ten and a girl who is seven years old. Liz has chosen to be a stay-at-home mother and has decided to home-school her children. She feels she can best support her husband and care for her family if she does not work outside the home. Her husband is the senior pastor of a large church and is frequently invited to speak at various seminars and conferences around the country and even around the world. He is gone a lot, but even when he is home he is so occupied with the demands of his job that Liz finds herself feeling very lonely. She has tried getting involved in the children's ministry at church, but finds it difficult to form close friendships with members of her church. She is guarded about her feelings and cannot confide her feelings to anyone at the church for fear of creating gossip about her husband and their relationship. She also does not want to confide in family members who may not be able to forgive her husband for the pain he is causing her. She has tried to let him know how she feels, but he insists he must keep up his schedule to support the family financially.

As we contemplate Liz's story, I would like you to think of a career that has no boundaries with regard to time. Consider one that might require being on call 24/7, where you can never completely unplug; always just a phone call or a text away from your next assignment. Such is the life of the pastor or minister of the Gospel. Liz's husband is not unlike many pastors. Their work is one of selfless service. They are expected to come whenever called; to a meeting, a personal emergency of a member or even a non-member of the church. They are expected to be present for the nodal events of people's lives: Their marriages, anniversaries, the birth of their children, at the hospital bed when someone is ill, or at the bedside when someone is dying. After all, this is the call of the pastor – to be present and supportive through these nodal events in people's lives. The woman who agrees to stand by his side is expected to support him as he fulfills these daily demands and expectations. Depending on the size of the church you are shepherding, these things can happen from time to time, or with great frequency.

The wife of the pastor can expect that at any moment, her husband can be called away. Much like an obstetrician who is on call and can be summoned at any moment to deliver a baby, the pastor is expected to attend to the personal challenges of the members of the church and the community. It can be anything, really. I recall my husband's phone ringing close to midnight one Saturday evening. It was a mother calling. She was worried about the whereabouts of her teenage daughter. Her daughter had apparently gone out with friends, but at this late hour could not be located. She was not with those friends she had left with a few hours earlier. It did not matter to this mother

11

what the pastor was doing, or that it was close to midnight on a Saturday night. He was expected to respond to her emergency right then and there.

At other times, it could be a phone call about a family member who is ill, perhaps just admitted to the hospital, or about one who has had a run-in with the law. Perhaps it's someone who has been evicted from his or her home, or the one who needs a letter or recommendation for school or work. It can be anything, and the call can come at anytime. The pastor's wife can usually understand these demands and emergencies, and will not hold them against her husband, since frequently she also responds to the needs of members in any way that she can; sometimes with prayer, a tangible gift, or just her presence to offer support.

But, the reality is that the demands on his time never stop. The pastor is expected to be wherever the church member needs him to be, and frequently he feels pressured to meet every expectation. It may be the usual church board meeting, or one of any other meetings held by members of the various ministries: Men's ministry, family ministry, elders' meetings, school board meetings; you name it. He is expected to attend and frequently he does. After all, this is his job and also his spiritual calling.

How about the counseling sessions for those in need of personal, marital or family therapy? This too requires much of the pastor's time and energy. Such sessions usually require odd hours such as evenings or weekends, when those being counseled are off from their jobs or have time to spare.

It is not uncommon for a pastor's wife to come home from her nine-to-five job (if she has one) to find her husband preparing to run off to a counseling session or meeting, leaving his wife and children all alone for dinner and evening activities.

This hectic and unpredictable schedule also makes planning vacations and personal time very challenging and difficult. Unless the pastor makes it a priority to block off personal time to be with his wife and family, it can be impossible to get him to totally unplug from ministry and attend to the emotional needs of his household.

Many pastors may or may not realize that taking care of their own marriage and family is in itself a ministry. For if he neglects his family, soon this will reflect negatively on him as a pastor, administrator and counselor. Some may ask, how can he help others with their personal and family issues if his is falling apart? How can he counsel the couple whose marriage is struggling, if his marriage is also on the brinks of failure? How can he minister to the parent whose child has gone astray, when his child is also ready to break away from the church? Pastors are expected to model the type of life they wish others to follow, or their words are considered to be empty syllables.

The purpose of this book is not simply to state the problem, but rather to offer the spouse of the minister tips and strategies for managing the challenges she faces. What should she do if her husband fails to prioritize the marriage and family? What should she do if she feels neglected? How can she handle the emotional and personal toll of being married to ministry? How should she approach the topic with her husband? Many pastors who are themselves counselors tend to be reluctant to seek help for their own marital problems, for fear of appearing to be incompetent in the very thing they seek to help others with. Should she just kneel in her closet and pray about it? Should she just hope he would somehow see that her needs are not being fulfilled and that she needs him to do a better job of balancing his career and marriage?

The fact is that the wife of the pastor frequently feels totally neglected as he attends to the day-to-day demands of his job. She is left alone to tend to her children and her household, while he attends to the needs of the church. The pastor's wife has to find a way to communicate her feelings to her husband; to let him know when she feels neglected; to tactfully get him to spend quality time with her and their children without making him feel condemned about doing the work he is called to do.

The children feel his absence as well. They can tell when daddy is gone too much; when he leaves for one too many speaking engagements, leaves to attend yet another meeting, or when he just cannot afford to sit with them at church or at home because he is busy with the affairs of his office.

So, what should she do when she feels neglected, or notices that her children are missing their other parent who is gone all too often? Following are a few suggestions to consider as you navigate the demands and challenges of being *the pastor's wife*.

Have the crucial conversation

Once Liz or any pastor's wife realizes that the demands on her husband's time are taking a toll on the marriage, it's time to have a serious talk about what's happening. Having the conversation may seem almost *too* simple, but this is where the solution starts. In the book entitled *Crucial Conversations*, the authors discuss tools for talking when the stakes are high. Though written as a business self-help book, the topic can be applied to any relationship that requires good communication to succeed. The first thing the pastor's wife should do is to communicate her feelings to her husband rather than avoid the topic. It is indeed possible that the pastor could be so preoccupied with doing his work for the Lord, that he does not realize that his spouse is feeling neglected. So, before resorting to any other strategy the pastor's wife should first let her husband know how she is feeling.

In our opening vignette, Liz is in a situation where her husband is busy doing the work of pastoring and traveling to do seminars; busy making money to support his family, while she is at home taking care of the household and the children. If she is feeling alone and neglected, it may mean there is something missing. The primary relationship is not receiving the attention it needs. She should find a suitable time to have a conversation with her husband about how she is feeling. Perhaps she can make a special dinner for just the two of them, and have a chat at that time. Or perhaps they can have the conversation during a brisk morning walk. In any case, the goal will be to utilize the opportunity to communicate how she is feeling. He may already be aware of her feelings, but she must not assume this. It's important for her to tell him.

Say it <u>nicely</u>

The second step is just as simple as the first but equally important. Remember that *how* you say something is as vital as what you say. The manner in which you have the conversation will make the difference between whether you achieve the outcome for which you are hoping, or whether it just turns into a useless argument that leaves your spouse feeling accused and defensive. In the case of Liz, here is an example of what she should not say: "Honey, I need to let you know that you are gone too much." While this is exactly what she is feeling, it might be perceived as being accusatory and would more than likely cause her husband to be defensive. The conversation may go a little better if she says something like: "Honey, the children and I miss you and want to spend more quality time with you." You might be able to understand how the second statement would be more palatable for the pastor to hear, and perhaps would generate a more beneficial outcome.

The point is that if Liz wants her husband to balance his work and home life better, she must have a constructive conversation with him about her feelings and needs as his wife and as the mother of his children.

Embrace his occupation

The pastor's wife is more likely to have a good relationship with her husband if she has a positive attitude towards the work he does. It is very easy for her to resent the work of ministry if she feels that it's taking her husband away. But, she must resist this temptation. She will do better if she embraces the reality of his demanding schedule rather than fight against it. She has to adapt her perspective and see his career for what it truly is. It's a call to care for the Lord's children, to win souls for Christ, and to nurture them as they grow spiritually. If she has a positive attitude about her husband's occupation, she will be more likely to support him fully, tolerate a few late-night meetings and out-of-town trips. She may even decide to join him on a few of his outings, or get involved in the ministry herself. If she is a stay-at-home mom like our friend Liz, she may be able to travel with her husband and take the kids along at times. After all, the pastor's wife is usually a God-fearing, bible reading, prayerful woman of God. She is not averse to the work her husband is doing. She simply needs him to balance his work and family life such that he does not neglect her or their children. She can help him do this by embracing his role and adopting a positive attitude. She can also embrace her role as his wife and help him to create a healthy balance serving as a minister, husband and father.

Embrace your role

Readily embracing your role can lead to achieving success and happiness in your marriage and family life. A positive attitude is more likely to generate positive results. Many pastors' wives may have their own profession outside of church work, but the role of being a pastor's wife is one she cannot ignore. Her role often requires supporting the pastor by working behind the scenes; aiding in his success. Yet, the role may not look the same for every pastor's wife, since each is unique and different. She may have certain talents or gifts that she can use in God's service alongside her husband. Perhaps she is a gifted pianist or soloist, who can take part in the worship service. Perhaps she has the gift of hospitality, and can host members of the church for brunch, lunch or dinner. Perhaps she has a gift for educating children, and she can play a role in the children's ministry. Perhaps she is a gifted speaker herself, and can speak to issues affecting women or children in the community. If she is an older woman, she may delight in mentoring younger wives, or other women in the church. There are varying opportunities for service and involvement. She must find her passion and make that her ministry. It would certainly enhance her husband's ministry if she also made use of her gifts and talents.

Join him

There is a common saying that goes something like this: "If you can't beat them, then, join them." There may be some wisdom to this. Instead of competing with the demands of your husband's job, why not join him when he goes off on one of his many pastoral visits or speaking engagements. Maybe he gets a call about a member who is ill and admitted to the hospital. If possible, try tagging along with him for the visit and joining him in ministering to the sick. The benefits to this strategy are tremendous. You will enjoy the blessing that comes with reaching out to serve the needs of others. It would also help you forget about your personal issues for a while, and afford you the opportunity to be with your husband as he ministers to those in need. You may find that this act of sharing in your husband's ministry serves to draw him even closer to you, as he will be grateful for your presence and support.

Pencil in your time and set boundaries

This approach serves really to help your husband prioritize his wife and family. At the start of each week, month or year, be proactive about setting aside quality time for the two of you, and for the children if they still live at home. Pastors and counselors already know the importance of spending time with their family, but may struggle with balancing the demands of ministry and the need to spend time at home.

Like other couples, the pastoral couple may need to prioritize a weekly date night or a summer getaway with the kids. Maybe a surprise birthday or anniversary present. Make it special and memorable; m ake it different. Something that will generate special memories for the two of you. Be sure to include him in the planning process if he is not fond of surprises. But, if he doesn't mind some spontaneity, make it an unexpected treat. You may need to solicit the help of influential others who can help to clear his schedule and eliminate a few tasks for the day. Maybe his associate pastor can take the pulpit for that weekend, allowing you and him to enjoy some guilt-free time together.

Find your own purpose

Maybe you are a stay-at-home mom, or perhaps you have chosen to pursue your career outside of the home. Either way, as a pastor's wife you know that supporting the pastor is a job in itself. It helps if you can find your own ministry to devote yourself to. Pick something you naturally enjoy. If you like working with children, get involved in the children's ministry. Perhaps you are passionate about women's issues. Then, women's ministry may be a good place to devote your time and energy. Maybe you work in the field of health or education. Your personal strengths and career can easily be applied to one of the ministries of the church, allowing you to have your own area of service to devote some time to. The benefits of selfless service will have many benefits for you both personally and spiritually.

The unpredictable and boundless demands of your husband's job do not need to put a damper on your relationship or on that of your family. It pays to embrace the reality of it all, and make the best of it. You can turn lemons into lemonade by adapting to the demands of ministry. Be creative in your approach. When things aren't going well, don't be afraid to let your spouse know how you feel. If he is thoughtful and prayerful, he will give you the time and attention you need. For if the pastor's wife is happy, the pastor will be happy too.

Partners in ministry

Couples in ministry often need the support of other clergy couples. They may be of the same age and stage of their career, or they may be older and more seasoned in the work of ministry. Either way, it helps if couples in ministry have other partners in ministry they can lean on for support, advice, prayer and counsel. Does your husband have a mentor? Someone he looks up to and admires, who is also a friend? This can be someone to lean on for support in difficult times. Every couple has their struggles and challenges. It would be very beneficial for both the pastor's wife and the pastor to have partners in ministry who can be counted on for constructive criticism and feedback, especially in the more trying times of ministry.

Seek professional help when needed

At times, despite all you have tried, it may still be challenging to rescue and nurture your relationship amidst all the demands of pastoral ministry. If you have tried communicating your feelings and feel that your needs are not being met, it may be helpful to seek professional counseling. This can be done alone or with your husband if he is willing to do so. Too often, couples see counseling as an admission of failure or weakness. But, it can be helpful to address the issues affecting the marriage or relationship before things become irreconcilable. Counseling may also help you and your spouse take steps to nurture your marriage and manage time in such a way that you do not lose touch with each other, as you serve the Lord.

Closing scripture:

"Behold I send you forth as sheep in the midst of wolves: Be ye therefore wise as serpents, and harmless as doves."

Matthew 10:16

Chapter 2:
Lonely in a Crowd

Maria is new at her current church. Her husband has been pastoring their new church for just six months. The members of the church have been friendly and kind toward her family, including her daughters, ages 7 and 12. But, Maria feels a bit isolated. She finds it difficult to form close friendships. She finds herself missing her former church family of 12 years and longing for the company of her old friends.

The inspiration for this chapter stems from the common experience often shared among pastors' wives. Despite being surrounded by people who may genuinely care for her and wish to befriend her, she may still feel very much alone and not know who to trust. There is a limit to how close she can become to members of the church. As the wife of the shepherd of the flock, her innermost feelings cannot be divulged to just anyone. Her circle must be small and trustworthy. Many will seek to get close to her for their own self-serving reasons. She has to be able to discern whom she can trust with her thoughts and feelings, and whom she should not. For this reason, her trusted friends are usually few and as a result, her world can be quite lonely.

The other reason for isolation is because the call of ministry many times requires the pastoral family to move to different churches, cities, states and even countries. This pulls the pastor's wife and family away from previously formed social and support networks. In many cases, the pastor's wife must move away from her close family and friends to support her husband in ministry. As a result, she may find it difficult to adjust to new environments, cultures and social norms.

The issue of trust is a major factor for the first lady. You see, she holds a position of great influence as the spouse of the minister of the church. She can potentially sway the pastor's hand one way or another, simply because she is his wife. Many know this, and will seek to draw close to her, if only to be able to tap into her powers of influence in their favor.

Then, there are others who are simply inquisitive. They want to know her business, and the personal affairs of the first family. They pride themselves with being in the know. So they gravitate to her, but with no genuine care or concern for her well-being or that of the family.

It is therefore important for the pastor's wife to develop a keen spirit of discernment in order to know whom to trust, and whom to keep at arm's length.

The pastor's wife must be careful to guard the secrets of her household, for fear of causing discouragement and disillusionment in those who put her family on a pedestal and expect nothing short of perfection. You see, the pastor's wife knows all too well that she is not perfect, nor is her husband or children. Yet, there are those who want them to be perfect, and don't know how to deal with the humanness of the pastoral family.

In one of our several churches, I would frequently be pulled aside by a well-meaning member who would report to me the shortcomings of one of my children. You see, my son is quite intelligent and has a mind of his own. He went through a stage of development where he absolutely resented being called the pastor's son. He would say, "My name is Anthony and I am not my father." He would speak up in bible studies, and at times could be a little insolent. I had one teacher say to me, "can you please speak to your son?" She pointed out that he did this or that, or was acting out in class. She was in disbelief that he could be acting out. After all, he is the pastor's son! Of course I would have a word with my son after church about the incident, but he would be very upset that people were always referring to him as the pastor's son, and would be shocked if he acted in any way outside of the angelic child they had expected. I would not condone any disrespectful behavior on his part, but I did understand his annoyance with those who felt the need to point out his position as the pastor's child, as if his behavior would be more acceptable if he were not the pastor's son.

Similarly, the pastor's wife frequently feels isolated due to expectations of her conduct. The expectations of many churchgoers can be quite detailed, from the way she should dress, wear her hair, educate her children, or where she should sit during church. Many want her to be a professional singer or pianist, able to accompany any musical piece on demand. Her children are expected to be well dressed and well behaved. If not, they feel that she is failing in her job as a pastor's spouse and as a mother.

These and other unrealistic expectations can leave the first lady feeling isolated, rejected and very much alone. If she doesn't fit the mold that some have created for her, they tend to reject her. Some would talk about her behind closed doors. Others will simply never talk to her, or avoid any interaction with her. So, how can she overcome this problem of feeling isolated though surrounded by many people?

Pray for wisdom

The first lady will need an extra dose of wisdom to know how to best navigate the waters of a new church family. As in the case of Maria, she needs to know how to respond to the expectations of others, demands on her time and complaints from well-meaning members about her children. She needs to know how to love people who may not be loving toward her husband and her family. She needs to know how to overcome the grips of loneliness that plague many ministers' wives, especially in a new church community. What better way to obtain wisdom, but through the power of prayer? She should pray for wisdom to help as she networks with her new church family. She should pray for discernment, to determine the genuine caring person, from the one who may be up to no good. She should pray for guidance to know how to best minister in her own way to those in the church and in the community. And yes, she should pray for her husband as he navigates his own struggles of adapting to a new assignment. She should also pray for her children; that their spiritual lives will be nurtured as they too adapt to a new place and new people. There is power in prayer, and it is no cliché to say that the first thing the pastor's wife ought to do is seek the Lord in prayer.

Join a support group for pastors' wives

There is no better place to feel safe to be yourself than among others who experience many of the same things you do. Joining a support group for pastors' wives will help the first lady remember that she is not alone. She can draw strength from the support of others who experience many of the same challenges as she does. She would still need to use her discretion to know how much to share in a group such as this, as some things may not be appropriate to discuss with ladies you may not know very well. I recently read a comment from a minister's wife who said she didn't feel safe to share at a pastors' wife retreat, because the other wives seemed to have it all together. The ability to share with others and be real about one's feelings will not work if the wives do not know and trust each other. The ability to share and discuss personal matters is only possible if the group is deliberate about creating a safe and confidential place where the spouses of pastors can be real, open and honest about their struggles and feelings, without having to worry about gossip or appearing to be weak. Read more about this in the chapter on *taking off the mask*.

Seek trusted mentors

The road we tread is not unique. There are always those who have gone before us. They've been where you are and can understand and empathize with what you go through. The pastor's wife should seek the wisdom and counsel of others who have been in the role for many years. The more seasoned pastors' wives can counsel the younger. They can share the wisdom they have acquired over the years, and help to guide the younger wives as they adapt to their role. The wisdom that accompanies experience cannot be underestimated. Once, while at an event for pastors' wives, there was an older woman whose husband had passed away years prior. She talked about how it was important to value your husband while he is alive and well. Too often, we do not miss the water until the well runs dry.

In other words, we fail to truly appreciate our spouses until they are no longer with us. Her council changed my perspective a bit, and helped me to appreciate my husband more, rather than complain about his shortcomings.

It may also help to have a few close friends with whom the pastor's spouse can share personal feelings or request special prayer. After all, she is human and the need for an outlet or just a listening ear can go a long way to alleviate loneliness and depression for the wife of the pastor.

Focus on others

Serving others is one of the best cures for loneliness and depression. It lifts you out of your troubles and reminds you that there are others facing far worse circumstances than your own. Not that you want to benefit from the misfortune of others, but there is a blessing to be had when you focus on helping others, rather than focusing on yourself. Service is a natural mood enhancer. Few things can bring inner peace and joy like serving the needs of another. For this reason, it would serve the pastor's wife well to find an area of service in which she is passionate. It should be something she truly cares about and that she would enjoy devoting time and energy to. It might be a ministry for children, teaching about health and wellness, arts and crafts, or maybe she is gifted with her hands or passionate about prayer and fasting. Whatever her source of interest, she can turn it into a ministry that can uplift and enhance the life of others. It is the best cure for loneliness and depression.

Our friend Maria was able to find this cure for her loneliness. She decided to be proactive about making new friends. So once each month she decided to host a Sunday brunch for the women of the church. She would host and each lady would bring a dish. Their children were invited as well, and she would be sure to provide a babysitter for the children, while the ladies got some time to chat with one another. Before long, Maria was feeling much more at home in her new church, as she formed new bonds of friendship with members of her church.

I have heard it said that in order to have friends, one must first be friendly. This sounds simple, but most certainly is true. The wife of the pastor will do well if she is intentional about reaching out to others and shows genuine interest in their well-being. Ultimately, if the wife of the pastor takes steps such as these; to reach and serve the people of her church and community, she will be able to escape the grip of loneliness, and feel more at home with the members of her church community.

Closing scripture:

*"A man who has friends must himself be friendly, but there is a
friend who sticks closer than a brother."*

Proverbs 18:24

Chapter 3:
Instability and Frequent Moves

Monique has recently learned that her husband was offered a job as the president and chief administrator of a university. It's one of the institutions of the church, and is a well-known church sponsored institution of higher learning. If he takes this position, she would have to leave her job. Her children will have to change schools. While she is happy for her husband and knows he may wish to accept this offer, she is not sure that this is the right time for the family to make such a move.

A common theme in the life of many pastors is the assignment from one church or congregation to another. In this case, Monique's husband is being offered an administrative role. The duration of the assignment is frequently unknown, but can vary from a few years to several decades. This brings a culture of uncertainty in the life of the pastoral family. Frequently without expectation, the pastor may be reassigned to another city, state or even country. If he is an administrator, his term may be limited as well, perhaps to a few years, and subject to the vote of his parishioners as to whether he would serve another term or be removed and replaced. The wife of the pastor would be expected to stand by his side and support his assignment, by leaving her job at a moment's notice; that is if she works outside of the home. She is often not able to advance much in her field of work, as she is not able to remain in one location for any significant length of time.

There are some pastoral families that choose to engage in mission work. They may relocate to a foreign country, usually in parts of the world that are less developed and have great need. The family may choose to spend several years in these mission fields even as they have children and deal with the demands of parenting. These assignments can be very fulfilling and rewarding for those who are called to this work.

In addition, the pastor may be called away from church service and into a more administrative role; perhaps leading other pastoral families, or entire church regions. These assignments can be very demanding on his time and energy. Again, the pastor's wife is expected to play a supportive role in any of these scenarios.

The point of these examples is to underline that the dreams and desires of the pastor's spouse are usually secondary to her husband's work assignment. That reality can leave her feeling unfulfilled. However, if the move is one that the pastor's spouse and family desire, then there is less of an issue or cause for conflict. Often, the wife is concerned about the welfare of the children. Depending on their stage of development, they may be more or less affected by the change. Are they happy at their current school? Do they want to move to another region, state or country? Will they like the new place? Will they adapt and make new friends? All these and other concerns will be on the mind of the pastor and his wife when a move is being considered.

Frequently, if the move is not one that the pastor's wife desires, or that the kids are looking forward to, there can be adverse consequences on their emotional and mental health. The pastor's wife can easily become anxious about the impending change, or she may become depressed. Signs of depression may include a lack of motivation or desire to do anything, trouble sleeping, fatigue, poor appetite or overeating. She may have trouble concentrating on her work. The same can happen to children, depending on their stage of development. Younger, elementary aged children are usually more flexible, resilient and able to adapt to change more easily. Older children who have formed close friendships either at school or in the community may find it more difficult to move away and leave their social network. Thankfully, there are some helpful tips that can make these transitions smoother.

1: Visit the new community before the official move

If at all possible, it may help for the family to visit the new community before the actual move. This holds true for any family that is moving to a new place. It may be helpful to check out housing and schools for the children. One may also want to explore some of the fun things to do in the new community. Perhaps they want to visit the new church and get a preview of what life would be like in the new community. It may help to explore the culture of the new church. What is their style of worship or dress? What are the expectations of the pastor's family? What are some of the needs of the church and the new community? Knowing these things could potentially ease some of the anxiety on moving day and actually give the family something to look forward to.

2: Keep in touch with friends and family

Moving away does not mean you can't keep in touch with family and friends. It is important to take steps to maintain these relationships. Of course, it won't be the same if you are moving a significant distance away. But today's technology including such platforms as Skype, Facetime and Facebook, allow for friends and family to keep in touch, despite the fact that you have moved away. A good old phone call doesn't hurt either. Once the move has occurred, it also helps to take a trip back from time-to-time, just to remind you that they are still there, and to reconnect and remember the good old days. Either way, you should strive to maintain old friendships and relationships, as you seek to make new ones, so as to nurture your social support network.

3: Pray for wisdom and guidance

I may have said this before. But one should never underestimate the power of prayer. It really helps to bring a sense of peace despite life's challenges and difficult circumstances. God says to us in Philippians 4: 6-7, "Be anxious for nothing, but in everything by prayer and supplication, with thanksgiving. Let your requests be made known to God. And the peace of God, which surpasses all understanding, will guard your hearts and minds through Christ Jesus."

Whatever causes you fear or anxiety; bring it to God in prayer. Include the children and encourage them to pray to God about any concerns they have about the move. In time, God has a way of working things out, so that the first family adjusts seamlessly to the new assignment.

4: Seek help if having trouble adjusting

This piece of advice is very important, more so for anyone struggling with the idea of moving. If there are serious signs that one is having trouble adjusting, then professional counseling may be necessary. These signs include trouble sleeping, excessive fatigue, poor appetite or overeating, little or no desire to do anything fun, trouble concentrating, and even thoughts of death or suicide. It is important to pay attention to these signs if they occur and take action to address them before they get worse. One may see a therapist or a medical doctor if these signs are present for any significant length of time.

5: Look at the bright side

In other words, see the glass as half-full. Moving can represent a positive change in the life of any family. It can be an opportunity to explore new things, to meet new people, make new friends and serve a new community. The first family has a unique opportunity to minister to the needs of many people when they enter a new community. They should see it for what it really is: An assignment from God to minister to a new community. They should not be like Jonah, who tried to run from God's errand. Rather, they should embrace the new opportunity and purpose to serve God with all their heart. Now, let's revisit the story of Monique:

After much prayer and soul searching, Monique whom we met at the beginning of the chapter, decided to support her husband in accepting his new job offer. Her children, who were still in elementary school, were sad at first to leave their friends, but after visiting the new community and their new home church, the children were able to see their new school, and mingle with some of the children there. They became excited about the future, and were able to adapt to their new home and school. Monique resigned from her job as a nurse, and was able to get a new job at a hospital in the new community. It seemed the transition was easier than

41

she had anticipated. She got involved with the health ministry at their new church, as well as the children's ministry with her kids. Their family was blessed by having made the move, that they believe was the will of God.

Closing scripture:

"The Lord will guide you always; He will satisfy your needs in a sun-scorched land and will strengthen your frame. You will be like a well-watered garden, like a spring whose waters never fail."

Isaiah 58:11

Chapter 4:

Issues Related to Finances

In my research on pastors' wives, another topic that came up as one of their unique concerns is that of inadequate finances. It was ranked very highly along with lack of time together and lack of personal friends. Historically, pastors have been compensated poorly compared with other professions. In a recent study, the Department of Labor Statistics indicated that of 432 occupations, clergy ranked 317 in terms of their earnings. While their educational level ranks them with the top earning occupations, their compensation is on par with that of unskilled labor. Part of the reason for this discrepancy has been the widely accepted thought that the pastor or minister is a servant of God, and that his earthly toil would be rewarded not in this life, but in the next.

This problem of inadequate compensation certainly has effects on the pastoral family and particularly on the wife. Though times are changing, she is still primarily responsible for hosting social engagements, decorating and upkeeping the home and serving lavish meals. The pastor's compensation also would affect what type of home the family is able to afford, as well as whether they can be financially supported during their retirement years. Due to these concerns, more and more clergy wives are having to seek employment outside of the home. This is necessary to make ends meet, to finance their children's education and to ensure greater financial stability for their later years.

The prospect of working outside of the home brings new complexity to the life of the pastor's wife. If she has her own career, she must juggle her role as the pastor's wife with that of her occupation. If they are also raising young children, this too adds much to the plate of the pastor's spouse. The demands of being a pastor's wife, a mother and a career woman would certainly increase her risk of burnout and fatigue. In my book *Achieving Balance: A Guide For Busy Working Mothers*, I give several tips on how working mothers can help to balance their roles at home and at work.

In today's world many women are pursuing terminal degrees and working in notable occupations. It is not unusual today to see pastors' wives who also have their own careers. Some are educators, nurses, doctors, and lawyers. Some choose to work full-time, while others may find that part-time work is much more manageable. Either way the pastor's wife, who also has an outside occupation, is certainly juggling at least two roles. The role of pastor's wife is conferred on her just because of the man she is married to, while she would also have to fulfil the role of her paid profession. There may be pros and cons to this situation.

Certainly, one of the benefits to having her own occupation is that she is no longer defined simply by her husband's career. She would have her own identity in her field of work. She would still have the role of pastor's wife, but can also make a contribution to society by working in her chosen field of study.

Another benefit to working outside the home is the additional income that she would be able to bring in, thereby contributing to the economic well-being of the family. She would be able to provide insurance for health, dental and counseling services, as well as provide income for her children's education and extracurricular activities. Thirdly, she would be ensuring better financial stability for her retirement years if she has and is pursuing her personal career.

The downside to her working would come with the physical demands of juggling work, parenting and supporting her husband in ministry. This would certainly affect her physical and mental health, and would increase her risk of fatigue and burnout. She may also face criticism by those who believe that her place should primarily be in the home and supporting her husband. I think that most pastor's wives would need to decide for themselves what would be best for them individually and for their families.

I personally work outside of the home as a physician, and have had to cut back my hours to achieve a better balance for myself and my family. But, it truly is a struggle and can take both a physical and mental toll. As part of my role in supporting my husband, we would host dinners at our home for visitors and members of the church. It is sometimes challenging to find the time to prepare meals and clean the house with such a busy schedule. In a Research article entitled, "His Job. Her Life; A survey of Pastor's wives", the following was noted:

> "Because the parsonage (or pastor's home) is often used for church meetings and other gatherings, her life is structured around his needs and the church's needs. Her home is always semi-public. Moreover, this creates more work for her because the house must always be clean and yet it is constantly being messed up by unscheduled visits. This is especially hard for women with young children and/or women who are employed outside the home."

Despite the struggles of juggling life as a mother, pastor's wife and career woman, I really would not change a thing. I feel blessed to be able to serve both in the church and in the community. Here are some of the tools that have worked for me to help maintain balance and sense of peace:

1: Get Help When Needed

I have found that there are those who are able and willing to help with household needs. If the pastor's wife has young children, the assistance of either her mother, or a hired mother's helper, can go a long way to help her manage her childcare duties.

I have also found that hiring help for housekeeping can be invaluable for the mother who is working full-time or part-time.

When the children are older, they can certainly help out with household chores. But one way to keep that sense of balance and avoid burnout is to get the help you need.

2: Know when to say "no"

Just because you are the pastor's wife, does not mean you have to hold an office in the church. There are many ways to contribute to ministry, without holding an official title or office. One of the things to note where saying "no" is concerned, is that pastor's wives come in different ages and stages. Some are newly married with no children. Some are recently married and raising elementary aged children. Some have older children who have left the nest, while others are grandparents and may also be retired. Depending on her are and stage, the pastor's wife may be at a place where she can contribute only a small amount to church ministry. As her children get older and more independent, she may be able to do more in church ministry. Once she has retired she may have more time on her hands to contribute to her church ministry. So, one does not need to feel guilty about saying "no" when necessary. This allows the pastor's wife to serve in the capacity that she is able depending on her age and stage of life.

3: **Ask for God's guidance**

I truly believe in the power of prayer and God's willingness and ability to lead us when we are in need of wisdom and guidance. His word tells us to "trust in the Lord with all your heart, and lean not on your own understanding; In all your ways acknowledge Him, and He will direct your paths." God knows what's best for us at any particular time. If we ask him, He will reveal to us how best to care for ourselves and for our families at any point in our lives.

Closing scripture:

"I can do all things through Christ who strengthens me."

Philippians 4:13

Chapter 5:
Great Expectations

The church often has great expectations for the first family, and certainly for the first lady. Much like the first lady of any great country, there are many expectations of the first lady of the church.

The term *first lady* is an unofficial title used for the wife of a chief executive. It is also used to describe a woman at the top of her professional art or field. First spouse can be used where the spouse of a head of state is either male or female. It is interesting to note that the term *first lady* is believed to have originated in the United States, where it was first used in 1838 in reference to Martha Washington.

So, how did this term come to be used in reference to the pastor's wife? Little is known about its origins in the church, but it is certainly a growing trend. It places her in a role that she usually does not request or desire, yet may feel the need to live up to. The first lady is expected to dress to impress, wear the best clothes and exquisite hairstyles. It is not unusual for churchgoers to examine her from head to toe as she walks into the church, commenting either positively or negatively based on their expectations of how she should dress.

She is also expected to be active in ministry; women's ministry, children's ministry, and hospitality to name a few. She is frequently expected to be naturally gifted with a beautiful voice and the ability to perform solo renditions on request, or she may be expected to be a gifted musician with the ability to play the piano, organ or other musical instrument.

Some expect her to host lavish dinners, complete with three or four course meals. Her children are expected to be well behaved and well mannered. She should be present for most events and support her husband in ministry at all costs. Such are the great expectations of the wife of the church's leader.

These expectations frequently put excessive pressure on the wife of the minister. She usually wants to attend church services for worship, support her husband and be active in ministry in the church. But, the unusual expectations of some can make her anxious about the expectations of many churchgoers. If she is unable to measure up in the eyes of some, she may be the subject of negative commentary or gossip. She may also be isolated or mistreated by some. I once encountered a pastor's wife who talked about how the role had caused her so much stress that she developed high blood pressure and major depression as a result. Like her, there are some who come to view attending church more as a chore rather than a joy. There is also those who simply rebel and do the very opposite of what is expected of them.

The truth is that there is no biblical mandate to have a role for the wife of the pastor. Her duty as his wife is to support him in ministry in the best way that she can, without having to live up to expectations that were not required or requested by the God we serve. So, here are some tips to help pastoral spouses navigate through the waters of the great expectations of others:

1: **Be your unique self**

God created only one you. That might seem like an obvious and simple statement, but it is nonetheless true. There is only one you, with your unique talents, gifts and abilities. Embrace that uniqueness, and feel free to be you. Too often others expect us to fill the shoes of one who has gone before. Perhaps the former pastor's wife was a gifted musician or singer. That does not mean you have to be. Find your unique gift, and use it for the glory of God in your unique way. Perhaps you are a teacher and you have the gift of teaching children. Therein lies your possible ministry and one of the ways you can serve in the church. Perhaps you have the gift of creativity, and you can make wonderful things with your hands. This could be your unique ministry that can be used to bless others. Perhaps you like putting pen to paper and expressing yourself in journals, articles or books. This could be your unique blessing to others. Break free from the confines of the box for pastors' wives and feel free to express yourself as you truly are.

2: **Learn to say "no"**

One of the ways others try to place us in their box of expectations is to ask us to play certain roles or do certain tasks that they think pastors' wives should do. They envision us in a particular role, perhaps because of prior experiences with other pastoral spouses. There may be an expectation that the pastor's wife should act as a co-pastor. Some expect her to lead out in one of several ministries. They may envision her as the head of women's ministry or children's ministry. Some may expect her to be involved with the music ministry or the choir. Once, there was a church that my husband began pastoring, and not long into his tenure I was approached by one of the ladies of the church and asked if I could play the piano. It so happens that I took piano lessons in my earlier years, but at the time I was very much out of practice and did not wish to make a public spectacle of myself by playing for the church and making mistakes. So, I tried to say with as much gracefulness as I could muster, that yes, I do play the piano, but not for church at this time. The lady was a bit disappointed and explained that she merely wanted to have some variety in the pianist for church each week. Apparently, they were tired of seeing the same people playing the piano each week. I stood my ground, and said I would be happy to serve in other ways, but not as the church pianist.

Many times, we need to resist the attempts of those who wish to make a public spectacle of the pastor's wife. It takes great courage to say no and to prevent others from making us into their image of what a pastor's wife should be.

3: Choose your ministry and give it your all

I am reminded of the text in the book of Ecclesiastes 9 and verse 10 that says "whatever your hand finds to do, do it with thy might…" In other words, whatever you feel inspired to do, give it one hundred percent of your effort and energy. In terms of church ministry, if the pastor's wife chooses to serve in a particular office or ministry, she should devote herself to it fully. Her dedication should be whole-hearted, and directed by her passion about her field of service. If she loves what she does, it will show and also bring her fulfilment and priceless blessings.

Instead of letting others define you, be proactive in choosing your ministry or area of service. The choice of ministry for a pastor's wife is dependent on a few factors, including her personal talents and gifts, her interests and passions. It is best if she chooses to serve in the area for which she feels best suited.

You may be a great pianist, singer, teacher, artist, or perhaps you feel called to minister to other women or families. The point is that you should do that which you are passionate about and do it with all your heart.

4: **Don't sweat the small stuff**

Remember that expectations are simply people's ideas of how they think you should be. Their expectations are limited by their own experiences and their view of the church and pastoral family. Do not take people so seriously that you begin to feel stressed, as this can negatively affect your health and well-being. It can also affect your ability to truly love and care for them. Remember that they are fallible human beings who may falter at times. It's best at times to overlook senseless comments and even hurtful words. As Jesus himself said when he lay hanging on the cross, as the Roman soldiers prepared to crucify him, "Father, forgive them, for they know not what they do." So, likewise, we ought to forgive people when they say and do things that hurt us. Your focus should be on supporting your husband, taking care of your children and your family. You should also serve the church in the way that you choose and try to reach only the expectations of God. Focus on being who you are, and doing what God sent you to do, and let others deal with *their* expectations.

Closing scripture:

"For I know the plans I have for you, declares the Lord, plans to prosper you and not to harm you, plans to give you hope and a future."

Jeremiah 29:11

Chapter 6:

Caring for the Children

This chapter focuses on the unique experiences of the children of pastoral families or pastors' kids, commonly referred to as PKs. These children share several unique experiences as they grow up in what may feel like a glass house. Some may describe it as living under a microscope. They are highly visible, thoroughly scrutinized and experience a unique popularity just by virtue of being the pastor's kid. Unfortunately, while these children are exposed to church and positive messages about God most of their formative years, the challenges they endure can many times lead them to rebel and leave the church and religion all together.

Like their parents, these children are usually placed on a pedestal. They are expected to be model children, and little room is allowed for childhood mistakes. Their misdemeanors are frequently reported to their parents, and to others who may have little or no significant relationship or interaction with the children. The excessive scrutiny and criticism can leave these children feeling angry and resentful toward church, if nothing is done about the negative experiences they endure.

Secondly, these children can also be adversely affected by the hectic schedule of their parents, particularly that of the pastor. He is frequently occupied with the demands of church work, and just as his spouse can feel neglected, so can the children. They would notice whether or not he picks them up from school, helps with homework, is physically and emotionally present at dinnertime, or helps with the bedtime routine. They are there when he takes one too many phone calls and when he is not really listening when they are trying to have some quality time with him. Indeed, the pastor may be physically present, but emotionally detached or absent if preoccupied with church and other affairs.

These children are also impacted by every move their pastoral parents make. When the pastor decides to take on a new assignment, the children usually have little choice in the matter. They are pulled away from friends and family, as they move from place to place, and church to church. Bonds that were formed are abruptly broken, and effort must be made to adjust and make new ones.

There is also the effect of negative commentary about their parents. As these children grow older, they observe the way others talk about their parents. Many people forget that children are listening and paying attention to what they are saying, and unfortunately, many church members do not think about the pastors' kids, when they engage in gossip or hurtful comments about their parents.

Finally, there is the attempt by some to impose their views on the pastor's children with regard to what are usually considered personal choices. Many church members are quick to comment on how these children should be educated, which if any schools they should attend, and what their field of study should be.

I share the experience of my son, who looks and acts very much like his father, so much so that people say to him that he should also be a pastor like his father. He responds very negatively to this implication as he feels that his personal choice or desire is often overlooked as many try to make him a clone of his father.

As parents, the pastor and his wife need to prioritize the health and happiness of their children. There are steps that can be taken to minimize the negative impacts of church work on their children, and ensure that their children accept the message they are attempting to give to others and not leave the church. I recall the words of Mark 8 and verse 36 that says: "For what shall it profit a man, if he shall gain the whole world, and lose his own soul?" In like manner, I would ask, what shall it profit a pastor, if he saves the whole church and loses his child?

Many Pastors are busy helping others, and attending to their needs, while their own children long for quality time and meaningful experiences with them. It is essential that pastoral parents strike the right balance between ministry and parenting. So, how can pastoral parents guard their children against the negative experiences of ministry and ensure a more positive experience for their children? Here are a few suggestions:

1: Spend quality time with the children

Both the pastor and his wife must be intentional about spending quality time with their children. Nothing lets them know how very important they are than to have the undivided attention of their parents. Set some rules for personal family time. For example, no cell phones at the dinner table. Inquire about their day, help them with homework and be fully engaged as you prepare them for bed each night. Family worship should be a regular occurrence, whether it's a nightly devotion before bedtime, or a weekly family worship at the end of each week. This should be a sacred time when discussions centered around blessings and challenges can be addressed. The parents must endeavor to be fully engaged and present during these precious moments with their children.

Family vacations and time away are also very important. The pastor and wife should be intentional about planning family getaways; perhaps a retreat or a short trip for the family to spend some uninterrupted time together. This would go a long way to let children know that they are valued and loved.

2: Build their self-esteem

It's important for pastoral parents to build their children's self-esteem. It's important to let them know how much they are loved, whether they are behaving nicely or whether they make mistakes. When others point out their shortcomings or misdemeanors, the parent must be thoughtful about their response. Rather than going to the child each time there is a negative report, it may help to have general discussions about what is considered to be acceptable and unacceptable behavior. Rather than saying, sister so-and-so said that you did or said something bad, talk about what the child did well that day. With any child, reinforcement of positive behavior tends to work better than too much attention placed on negative behaviors.

3: Involve them in ministry and significant decisions

Even though the children have little say in the movement from one church to another, parents usually consider the impact the move will have on them. Depending on their age and ability to understand what is happening, involve the children in decisions that are made. Talk with them about their feelings and thoughts about a particular move. Get their perspective on challenges that arise, how they feel about leaving friends and family, and how they can keep in touch. Stay in touch with their feelings and attitudes about how things are going. Depression among teenagers is now so common that all children between the ages of 12 and 21 must be screened for depression. Parents need to pay attention to any signs of depression in their children. Are they isolating themselves or not wanting to do much with others? Are they having trouble sleeping? How are they doing at school? Do they have trouble concentrating on schoolwork? Are their grades dropping? Are they spending an excessive amount of time confined to their rooms and on screens? If these signs are noticed, it is important to get the children the help they need. They may need focused prayer and fasting. It may also be necessary to seek professional counseling or schedule a visit to the family doctor or pediatrician. Indeed, it is important for pastors and their wives to be intentional in the care of their children, and not neglect their parental duties as they care for the church.

Involvement in ministry is also a very powerful tool to keep the children engaged with church work and spiritual things. It is certainly true that the more involved they are with church activities, the more likely they are to make friends and build meaningful relationships. Activities like choir and involvement in different clubs can nurture their talents and abilities as well as aid in their spiritual growth. When my son was just about to celebrate his twelfth birthday, he was nominated to serve on the media team at our church. He was very excited about this opportunity as he had a keen interest in technology. It is without doubt that his involvement in this ministry would bring new energy and interest in going to church by allowing him to serve in a meaningful way.

4: Enhance their positive experiences

Most pastors' kids will have some challenges, but they will likely have some positive experiences as well. It is important as parents to enhance the positive experiences our children will have as it relates to church life. As pastors' kids, they may have unique opportunities to travel and meet other children around the world. They may have opportunities to engage in mission work as they travel with their parents in various mission fields. It would be wise for the pastor and his wife to expose their children to the needs of children less fortunate than they are. Perhaps they can allow them to help these children in some tangible way; by sending letters, needed items of clothing or school supplies to kids who have a need. They can be encouraged to pray for these children on a regular basis, and pray for their needs.

Mission work does not have to be done overseas. Children can be encouraged to serve in their own hometowns or in some meaningful way in their community. They can get involved in feeding the homeless, especially the children, or in adopting a street that needs regular upkeep or cleaning. By involving the children in these self-less acts of service, they can grow to love ministry and service, thereby growing closer to the Lord.

Closing scripture:

"Train up a child in the way he should go; And when he is old, he will not depart from it."

Proverbs 22:6

Chapter 7:

Caring for Your Spouse and Your Marriage

Your husband may be the pastor of a church, or the chief administrator of a great institution, but he is still your husband and companion through life. The demands on his time and energy will be great. He will be under a lot of pressure to fulfill the expectations of others and will be at risk for physical, emotional and mental burnout. As such, it is important to take steps to care for him physically, mentally and spiritually. One of your roles as his wife is to encourage him to take care of himself and to strike the right balance between his work as a pastor and his roles as husband and father. Due to the many demands on his time and the lack of structure of his job requirements, it may be difficult for him to set boundaries that would protect his personal and family time. This is where he will need your help to prioritize the marriage, to balance the demands of his pastoral or administrative duties, and to nurture your relationship with him and not let the demands of pastoring take away from the time you ought to be spending with each other.

It is very typical at times for those who care for and nurture others to sometimes neglect their own needs. Christians in particular are accustomed to the notion of selfless service. We are led to believe that service for God means sacrificing much of our own needs. On the contrary, I believe that God expects us to care for ourselves even as we serve him and minister to others. In our biblical text, 3 John

2 says, " Beloved, I wish above all things that thou mayest prosper and be in health, even as thy soul prospereth."So, how can you care for your husband mentally and emotionally? I offer the following suggestions:

1: Take vacations

In most other professions, vacations are highly encouraged in order to avoid burnout. Some refer to it as a mental break or just time away with the family. When one fails to balance work and personal life well, they can suffer from various forms of mental illness. Mental and emotional illness may manifest in the form of stress disorder, anxiety, depression and burnout. Due to the nature of work that pastors do, they can easily get burnt out if they fail to take time to rest and spend quality time with their wives and families. They have to be able to unplug from their daily responsibilities at some point, or they begin to lose touch with their spouses, their children and even their own spiritual lives. To avoid burnout, the pastor and his wife need to set some boundaries around their time. They must prioritize their time together by scheduling regular date nights, planning vacations as a couple or as a family. To be successful at this, it is essential to first let the church or congregation know when they will be gone and have someone else in place to handle the work affairs in your absence. Certainly, a deacon, elder or fellow pastor can cover the church work while the pastor takes some time away with family.

By letting members know that you will be away and having plans in place to cover your phone calls and other demands, the pastor and family can then unplug from the phone calls and really enjoy some guilt-free time together. The church members will know that the pastor will be unreachable at that time, but will have assurance that someone will be in place to answer their calls if necessary. This also serves as an example to other couples and families in the church; showing that it is okay and highly recommended to take some time away.

2: Be his shoulder to lean on

Bill Withers wrote the song *Lean on Me* in 1972 that was featured in a film by the same name in 1989 starring Morgan Freeman. The song lyrics feature the popular line, "We all need somebody to lean on." This is certainly true for anyone, but also for great leaders, administrators and pastors. Even great presidents have advisors and trusted mentors. As the pastor's spouse, you should be his chief supporter and advisor. Being in a position of leadership and authority brings with it great mental and emotional stress. It can also be a lonely place with few close and trusted friends. While pastoring can be a rewarding and fulfilling career with many positive rewards, it can also bring emotional turmoil and stress. He has to deal with dissenting views when some do not approve of his job performance or how he manages administrative affairs. There is political infighting that can occur during and after meetings. Dealing with these and other challenges on a regular basis can contribute to mental and emotional illness.

As pastors' wives, we need to ensure that we create a nurturing environment for him at home. While we may not be able to change the circumstances creating tension or conflict, we can certainly provide a listening ear, words of encouragement, and a partner for prayer.

3: Encourage good healthcare

The pastor's physical health can also be affected by his job. If he is constantly on the go, and trying to meet many demands, the stress of the job may lead to medical problems such as high blood pressure, which can increase his risk for heart disease and other ailments. The pastor's wife should encourage him to schedule medical checkups at regular intervals to keep abreast of his physical health. He should know whether his weight, blood pressure and blood sugar are in a healthy range. He should be doing regular screening exams to detect things like prostate and colon cancer early. Prostate cancer now affects 1 in 6 men in the United States of America. Colon cancer is diagnosed in 140,000 people and causes 50,000 deaths annually. The pastor would be setting a good example for other men in the church by getting screening tests for prostate and colon cancer and letting them know about its benefits.

It is also important for the pastor to be eating a healthy diet. His wife can ensure that healthy food choices are made. A diet that is plant based and rich in the fruits and vegetables that God instructed us to eat, will go a long way to preserve the physical health and strength of the pastor and his family.

Another way that the pastor's family can model good physical health is to exercise together. One of the times I enjoy most with my husband is when we take an early morning walk together, sometimes by ourselves and at times with the children. It is an awesome way to spend time together doing something that benefits our physical health and well-being.

4: **Pray with and for your spouse**

The pastor's spiritual health is also at risk when he is overworked and not balancing things well. Studies have shown that many pastors may only spend time in God's word when they are preparing a sermon. It is important for the pastor and his wife to spend time in personal devotion, bible study and prayer, so as not to lose touch with the God they believe in and serve. The pastor's wife should also uplift her husband in prayer. It is important to lead the family in worship on a regular basis, so as to keep the spiritual connection with God as a family. During family worship we can praise God together for his many blessings, and request strength and wisdom to serve Him in a way that is pleasing to Him. It is certainly true that the family that prays together has a better chance of staying together.

5: Seek spiritual mentors

A mentor is defined as an experienced and trusted advisor. Having a mentor can be very beneficial to people at various stages of life. It can also be helpful for the pastoral couple. Those who have been working in ministry for a longer time, would have words of wisdom and counsel for the younger minister and his family. They can serve as spiritual mentors, prayer partners, and counselors during difficult times. If the pastor is struggling with discouragement or temptation, a pastoral mentor can offer counsel and prayer. Perhaps, there are issues in the marriage, or things are just not going well, the minister and his wife can call on trusted mentors to guide them and pray for them in such times of need.

By taking care of our spouses and our marriages in this way, we are setting a good example for other families in the church. As they see us making time to be with each other, they too will prioritize their marriages and families and follow our example. By nurturing ourselves mentally and emotionally, we will be better able to care for those in our congregation and communities, and avoid the perils of stress, burnout and depression. By ensuring to keep our spiritual connection with God, we are able to serve God more fully, and better able to minister to those we lead.

Closing scripture:

"For this reason a man shall leave his father and mother and be joined to his wife, and the two shall become one flesh."

Ephesians 5:31

Chapter 8:
Caring for Each Other

Pastors' wives ought to care for each other.

The story is told of a minister's wife who felt very lonely after moving to a new church. She had a good marriage, but aside from her husband, had few people she could really confide in. She was very friendly with the members of her church, but still felt a void. She lacked the joy of true sisterhood, and felt there were few people she could really be herself around. She decided to join a pastors' wives group that met once a quarter at one of the local churches, and kept in touch online on a social network platform. She soon found that this was a wonderful way to make new friends and be of service to other women facing similar situations as her own. Before long, she was able to form meaningful friendships with several ladies from the group.

Much of what I have described in this book are experiences many clergy wives share from time to time. The feeling of being married to a man with an unpredictable work schedule, having to deal with poor boundaries between the church family and her nuclear family, having to protect her children from over-critical onlookers, and feeling alone at times even though she is surrounded by many people. These and other experiences are typical for many pastoral and administrative spouses. We can do a lot more to help each other by caring for and supporting each other.

Pastors' wives support groups

Every conference or union of churches should invest in a support group for pastors' wives. The purpose of the group would be to create a safe and nurturing environment for ministerial wives to share their joys and challenges with each other, and to support each other. This would require the women to first get to know each other on a personal level. This can be accomplished by engaging in fun and light-hearted social activities. Such activities can include brunches and dinners, spa dates, book clubs and much more. This would help to build trust and stronger relationships among the ladies, who would then be more comfortable to share with each other and depend on one another for emotional support.

My husband and I once served at a very large church in Southern California. We were blessed to have four or five pastors serving at one time. In order to get to know each other better, we thought it would be a good idea for us to have lunch together on a regular basis. We would meet at one of our homes together with our children and extended families. These occasions allowed us to spend time with each other, eat and talk together and share our experiences with each other. Our children enjoyed getting to know their fellow PKs and we were able to bond in a way that enhanced our working relationships.

I am not suggesting that pastoral families ought to isolate themselves and not fellowship with others. Certainly, they will continue to build relationships with others, and support the needs of others within the church. But, there is a need for pastoral families to support each other in ministry, because it can be a very demanding and challenging job that can hardly be understood or remedied by those they serve.

I also think pastors' wives especially need a safe space to voice their concerns, challenges and struggles in ministry. It is expected that they should wear a mask of perfection, always smiling and acting like all is well. I think this façade only contributes to that sense of loneliness we discussed before. If a pastoral spouse feels like other clergy wives have it all together and she is unique in her struggles, she is likely to keep her trials to herself and suffer with her challenges alone.

Before I say more about pastors' wives supporting each other, I would like to tackle one elephant in the room. That is, pastors' wives have been informally trained to keep their guard up, even among other clergy spouses. The same reasons she hesitates to share her innermost feelings with others will cause her to hide her feelings from her sisters in ministry as well. She fears that her secrets will not remain in confidence, and others will simply gossip about her. For this reason, often pastors' wives clubs end up being mutual admiration societies, where wives attempt to impress each other and show off how well they are doing, rather than admit to their shortcomings and struggles.

The other extreme is just as bad. This is, where the pastors' wives group becomes a pity-party, where the spouses use the opportunity to complain about their plight and spread negative stories about the people they are called to serve. This also is useless, and will have no positive impact on those within the group.

One other pitfall that can befall support groups for pastors' wives is the formation of cliques and subgroups within the larger group. These women might favor each other due to some common areas of bonding, and then may exclude others who don't fit into the group. This is not Christ-like and undermines to purpose of forming a support group in the first place.

I once attended a gathering of pastors' wives at a conference retreat. It was my first time being at a retreat for pastors' wives in this particular conference. I sat at a round table with about six other ladies, and across the room I could see that one of the other wives was looking intently at me. I was not sure why, but once we got the opportunity to move around the room and greet each other, she came directly to me and introduced herself and asked me my name. She asked how my family was and she specifically asked about my children. Her interest led me to reveal in just a few seconds that I was struggling with an issue with one of my children. It turned out that she had studied child psychology and offered to help me with the issue I was having with my child's behavior. We exchanged numbers, and even after leaving the conference, kept in touch with each other. The point of sharing the experience is that much can be gained if we are intentional about reaching out to others and show genuine interest and care about the lives of other pastoral spouses. We need to rejoice with each other in good times and support each other in the more challenging times of life. In order for this to happen, we need to do what that pastor's wife did for me at that conference. We need to be intentional about getting to know one another. We should show genuine interest in the lives of our sisters, and display the care and compassion that so many of us desperately need.

Another option that may work for some is to join an anonymous group that shares some common need. In this day and age when social media is so popular, one can find support groups online on places like Facebook and Instagram. On Facebook in particular, one can find support groups for single mothers, career mothers and certainly clergy wives. One benefit of this option is that it does allow for some privacy and anonymity, while still allowing women to share their feelings and seek words of encouragement and guidance from others.

In other cases we can be helpful to one another through prayer and fasting. We can start a prayer line or group telephone call where spouses can pray for each other's needs and requests. They can share bible verses to encourage each other if that is desired. If the prayer line is held at a consistent and convenient time, it can be a great source of strength for those who would prefer to stay within the privacy of home while connecting with other women for mutual encouragement and support. They can pray for their children and their spouses, and offer words of comfort and support when necessary. You would be surprised how many clergy wives are yearning for someone to care about them, and to be willing to take the time to pray with and for them.

We don't always manage to get this close to each other. We live in a world that is becoming a lonely place, not just for pastors' wives, but for people in all walks of life. As social media blossoms, people talk less. They don't reach out and touch as much. They don't look each other in the eyes and connect. They fiddle with their phones as if there is someone in there who can supply their needs. We can overcome this self-inflicted loneliness by making an effort to truly connect with one another.

Regardless of what path one chooses, pastoral spouses should endeavor to support each other and rally around each other in good times and in bad. By so doing, they will be showing the love of Christ and building a strong support network for the spouses who support the pastors.

Closing scripture:

"Bear ye one another's burdens, and so fulfill the law of Christ."

Galatians 6:2

Chapter 9:
Caring for You

Mrs. Carter presents to her doctor accompanied by her adult daughter. Mrs. Carter is now 60. She is married to the pastor of a large church in the community. Her daughter is 38, and accompanied her mother to her appointment because she is concerned about her mother's health and wants to make sure she tells the doctor everything that has been happening. Prompted by her daughter, Mrs. Carter reveals that over the last six months, she has not been sleeping well, she does not have much of an appetite, and as a result she has been losing weight without really trying. She feels tired most of the time and has no desire to do much. She forces herself to go to church. The doctor reviews Mrs. Carter's vital signs and notes that her blood pressure is 180/110 (normal for her is less than 140/90). Mrs. Carter admits having occasional headaches, but otherwise says she feels fine. When asked about her diet, Mrs. Carter says she eats a pretty healthy diet and goes for walks when her daughter asks her to. When asked if she is feeling stressed or if anything is bothering her, she then reveals that she is a pastor's wife, and things are not going well for her at their current church. Her husband is frequently criticized and talked about, and she feels as if the members of her church do not appreciate her, as she is not living up to their expectations.

Mrs. Carter's story is certainly not unique to pastors' wives, but is an example of what can happen when things are not going as well as expected with the current church assignment. Adverse relationships or political tension at a church can take a toll on the pastor and on his wife. Chronic stress can lead to several health issues such as depression and high blood pressure. Untreated high blood pressure can then lead to heart disease, kidney failure and strokes. It is important for the pastor's wife, who is charged with the care of the pastor, her children and the church family, to prioritize her health. If she does not, the results can be devastating.

As in the case of any spouse, the pastor's wife supports her husband in ministry, and she also cares for the well-being of her family. Her husband depends on her to be there for him, to support him, and care for him in good times and in bad. She also cares for their children who depend on them both to be good parents and to train them for life's challenges. It is therefore important for the pastor's wife to be in good health, physically, mentally and spiritually.

Too often, we see women and some men, committing to the care of others, but neglecting their own care. This is not wise, as it puts the caregiver at great risk for poor health, which eventually will limit his or her ability to continue to be of service to others. It's the philosophy of putting on your own mask, before seeking to help others. The pastoral family should be an example of good physical, mental and spiritual health, so that those they lead and serve can seek to do likewise. They can only do so if the chief caregiver is intentional about caring for his or her own health.

Physical Health

In terms of her physical well-being, the pastor's wife should first ensure that her diet is healthy. She should endeavor to prepare healthy meals, so as to nourish herself and her family according to God's will. In the book of 1 Corinthians 6: 19-20, we are told, "know ye not that your body is the temple of the Holy Ghost which is in you, which ye have of God, and ye are not your own? For ye are bought with a price: therefore, glorify God in your body, and in your spirit, which are God's." In the book of Genesis, we are told what God's original intention was for man's diet:

"And God said, Behold, I have given you every herb bearing seed, which is upon the face of all the earth, and every tree, in the which is the fruit of a tree yielding seed; to you it shall be for meat." This is found in the book of Genesis, chapter 1 and verse 29. In other words, God intended for us to eat a plant-based diet. It is still the best diet to promote health and prevent disease. Clergy wives should endeavor to prepare healthy, tasty meals for themselves and for their families in order to keep them healthy and strong, and to preserve good physical health.

Exercise is another important element of good physical health. The pastor's wife should be sure to take time to exercise and encourage her family to do the same. Most doctors recommend at least 150 minutes of aerobic activity each week. For example, one can do this in 30-minute sessions, five days per week or 50-minute sessions, three days per week. She should tailor her exercise to things she will enjoy doing. If the gym environment works for her, then joining a gym and exercising regularly is a good thing. Some may prefer the outdoors. A brisk walk outdoors, amid the fresh air, surrounded by trees and flowers are great backdrops to any exercise routine. Studies have shown that exercising outdoors can help to reduce depression and boost self-esteem. One should make it fun and relaxing, something you would look forward to doing each day. Perhaps she can encourage her husband and children to join her, thereby encouraging healthy habits that the whole family can enjoy.

She should be sure to schedule her routine medical and dental appointments at regular intervals, and get her blood tests and physical examinations so as to keep abreast of her health. Heart disease is the leading cause of death for women in the United States. It is estimated that 1 in every 5 female deaths are linked to heart disease. The risk factors for heart disease include uncontrolled high blood pressure, physical inactivity, uncontrolled diabetes, uncontrolled stress, depression and anger. The wife of the pastor should endeavor to maintain a healthy blood pressure, blood sugar and weight and limit her risk for disabling and life-threatening disease. By so doing, she can prevent disability, and preserve her quality of life and her ability to care for her family, and contribute to ministry in the church.

I would be remiss if I left out cancer screenings. Depending on her age and family history, she ought to get her regular screening exams for the early detection of cervical, breast and colon cancer. Research shows that 1 in 8 women will be diagnosed with breast cancer in her lifetime. It is the most commonly diagnosed cancer in women. Early detection can lead to easier, less invasive treatments and prevent untimely death. The same is true for colon cancer. She should get her colonoscopy, starting usually around age 50. She may need to do it sooner if she is at high risk. She should definitely be talking with her doctor about her risk for these cancers and when would be the best time to start screening for them. It would be a powerful testimony if she and her husband would do these tests and let the church membership know about it, thereby setting good examples for the entire congregation.

Mental Health

Her mental health is also very important. She should be on guard for signs of stress, burnout and depression. A short temper, mood swings and irritability may indicate a need to take a break. Not wanting to attend church may also be a sign of burnout and poor spiritual and emotional well-being. Perhaps it's time for a vacation or a weekend getaway with her husband. But, she may also need professional help if her symptoms are not improving.

It is important to know the signs of depression and be willing to seek help should the need arise. Our story about Mrs. Carter demonstrates several of the signs and symptoms of depression. Is she feeling down and depressed most of the time? Does she not want to get out and do anything fun? Does she not want to go to church? Is she having trouble falling asleep or staying asleep? Is she feeling tired all the time? Having trouble concentrating at work? Does she have a poor appetite, or is she overeating? These are some of the signs that she may be depressed. The ultimate symptom of depression is the feeling that one may be better off dead, and having thoughts and ideas of how they can take their own life. Suicidal thoughts are a sign of serious depression and warrant urgent intervention and treatment.

Mental illness can also take the form of anxiety, which can manifest as constant worry about things that are beyond our control. One may also have panic attacks which can cause heart palpitations, trouble breathing, trouble sleeping, racing thoughts and thoughts of doom that come without warning. While anxiety can be normal in stressful situations such as test taking and public speaking, it can be harmful when the feelings become excessive, and interfere with daily living. The bible tells us that we ought not be in a state of anxiety. In the book of Philippians 4 and verse 6, we are told: "Be anxious for nothing, but in everything by prayer and supplication, with thanksgiving, let your requests be made known to God; and the peace of God, which surpasses all understanding, will guard your hearts and minds through Christ Jesus."

At times, despite this knowledge, the pastor's wife may still feel anxious, perhaps about things she can't control. She should seek the counsel of a professional Christian therapist if these feelings persist or become unbearable.

Therapists are able to offer a non-biased and non-judgmental assessment of your situation. They can also offer several practical, but powerful tools to help in time of need. For example, one technique to deal with stressful times is journaling. This is the art of writing down your thoughts, especially when you have a lot on your mind. This and many other techniques can help the pastor's wife maintain a sense of peace and emotional well-being.

Spiritual Health

With regard to spiritual health, it is important for the pastor's wife to have her own daily time for prayer and devotion. She should study God's word daily for the spiritual food to face life's battles. At times she may need to engage in prayer and fasting. There are certainly times when we need to do both to get the results and answers to prayer that we need.

As in the case of Mrs. Carter, there are times when things may not be going well for the pastor's wife, the marriage or the family. They are human beings who are subject to failure and imperfection just like any other family. They live very public lives and usually are the center of attention. Thus, it may be difficult when problems arise in the marriage, or perhaps problems with the children to deal with these issues without feeling like the world is watching. It may be challenging to maintain one's privacy and deal with these issues. The need to fulfill the expectations of others can lead to stress and depression for the pastor and his wife in times of adversity. In times like these, close friends and family can be a source of support. Trusted friends in ministry can be a source of council and guidance. Members of the church should also pray for the pastor and his family on a regular basis.

Forgiveness

Before I close this chapter, I will place special emphasis on a practice that God encouraged; that I believe will especially benefit the wife of the pastor. This is the practice of forgiveness. The word *forgive* means to stop feeling angry or resentful toward someone for an offense, flaw or mistake. In your role as the pastor's wife, there are those who will offend you either in word or deed. It may be a member of the church. It may be someone you considered to be a friend. It may even be your husband. When we are wronged by another person, we feel wounded; we feel hurt; and it may be difficult to let that thing go. But if we are able to forgive those who have offended us, it is one of the most liberating acts we can perform both for ourselves and for the one who has offended us.

Jesus himself said, when he hung on the cross, "Father, forgive them; for they know not what they do..." He set for us an example of how we ought to deal with feeble men and women, who may do and say things to hurt us. Moreover, God says that we ought to forgive others, just as he has forgiven us. It can be a hard thing to do. But, if we as pastors' wives are able to extend forgiveness to those who have wronged us, it will free us from harmful negative feelings, and help us to be healthier physically, mentally and spiritually.

Closing scripture:

"Beloved, I wish above all things that thou mayest prosper and be in health, even as thy soul prospereth."

3 John 1:2

Chapter 10:
Taking Off the Mask

In my research on the wearing of masks, I found many interesting reasons why people wear masks. Regular masks are used commonly for utilitarian reasons, such as protecting one's face from pollution or dust. Some wear them to keep from getting sick or to prevent allergic reactions and colds. But more interestingly, people wear emotional masks. They wear them to hide what they are truly feeling. In some cultural backgrounds, it is not acceptable to openly express one's emotions. So the mask is used to keep them concealed.

It's even more intriguing that some people wear masks to hide their personality. This is referred to as a process called masking. Masking is defined as a process in which an individual changes or "masks" their natural personality to conform to social pressures, abuse and/or harassment. It's unfortunate that this process of masking often takes place in the church, because people feel the need to conform to social pressures or expectations in order to be accepted, to avoid criticism or even abuse. These same pressures can cause pastor's wives to wear masks. Societal pressures may cause the pastor's wife to feel the need to conform to people's expectations regarding several aspects of her life. There may be pressures to conform to a certain style of dress, a certain way to wear her hair, where she sits at church, and how she should behave. Some have expectations as to how she should speak, what talents she should have, and even what ministries she should either participate in or lead.

In many cases, these expectations are driven by cultural norms and experiences. There are some pastors' wives who fit the mold of people's expectations. They look exactly like the women on the cover of this book. They wear the fancy suit, with the matching hat, purse and shoes. Depending on the culture and climate, they may have gloves, stockings and other accessories to match. When church members get used to seeing women and especially the pastor's wife dress this way, they may expect it of all pastoral spouses. If one does not conform to this particular expectation, the pastor's wife may be shunned or even rejected.

The same goes for the way she comports herself. There are some pastor's wives who are very extroverted. They may enjoy being the center of attention, being around a lot of people, comfortable hosting dinners and parties. These women may be extremely confident, sit at the front of the church where they can be seen and heard, and take every opportunity to be in the spotlight. Meanwhile there are those who are no less confident, but a little more reserved, quiet and not so much in the spotlight. These women would rather not be so visible, but may be more comfortable playing a supportive role from the background. She may be the one who prepares meals at home and invites visitors. Or perhaps she contributes to meals served at the church. Perhaps she helps with bible studies and witnessing, or she may be more comfortable working with the children or youth ministries. The point is that one is not right and the other wrong. The pastor's wife should be free to be herself and not conform to being a certain way. She shouldn't have to conform to what I choose to call *the pastors' wives box*. She should be herself, still with appropriate dress and decorum, but very much herself.

To better illustrate the point, I will share the story of a first lady whom we will call Silvia:

Ms. Silvia is a young and spirited lady. She is attractive and talented and she loves the Lord. She caught the eye of a young pastor in training while they were both in college. Years later they got married and started a family. When they were assigned to their first church located in the South USA, the church folk were taken aback by the young couple, especially the pastor's wife. She wore her hair in its natural state, wore dresses with her arms exposed and refused to ever sit at the front of the church. She had young children at the time and felt much more comfortable sitting in the mother's room or at the back of the church, where she could attend to the needs of her children without causing too much distraction. Many had things to say about Ms. Silvia. She was nothing like her predecessor, who was quite the first lady; let's call her Mrs. Velda. You see, Mrs. Velda dressed to impress every time she came to church. It seemed she had an unlimited wardrobe that matched

*that of the queen of England. For every outfit, she had matching
hats, handbags and shoes. She wore her hair in traditional form,
and as she grew older, resorted to wearing a standard wig. Mrs.
Velda had her seat at the front of the church and would accompany
her husband as he walked in and out of the church. At times she
would even preach. Many of the members adored her as she fit the
mold of what a pastor's wife was expected to be. She was more
readily accepted, especially by the older generation in the church.*

Don't get me wrong, there is nothing wrong with the
way Mrs. Velda carried herself. There is much to be said
about having dignity and decorum. But that does not mean
that every first lady or pastor's spouse ought to carry herself
that way.

The way a woman dresses is based on so many
factors: Her age, culture, upbringing, personal sense of style
and comfort, her husband's preferences and her religious
beliefs. I believe there is room for variation based on these
factors, while still allowing a woman to dress appropriately
for her role. I believe it's possible for a woman to hold on to
her individuality, while still dressing and comporting
herself appropriately for her role as a pastor's wife.

Masking is not simply about dress. It's also a
question of personal gifts and talents. In today's world,
women have many choices. Gone are the days when women
were expected to stay at home and take care of the home,

and depend completely on her husband for financial support. Today a woman has the ability to choose to stay at home, or to choose to be gainfully employed outside of the home. Either path is appropriate. Yet, there are those who would try to make women believe that one way is right and the other wrong.

I believe a woman should choose to do what is best for her family, her well-being and her happiness. She may have pursued a formal education, but chooses to stay at home while her children are young. There is nothing wrong with this. Likewise, she may be the woman who chooses to nurture her career even as she raises her children. This too is perfectly fine. The woman who chooses to balance her career and raising her children can do so with the appropriate support and encouragement.

I know of many pastors' wives who choose to stay at home, work part-time or work full-time. They do what's best for themselves and for their families.

Masking may also manifest by the choice of ministry the first lady chooses. She may be gifted in a particular area, but feel pressured to conform to stereotypical ideas of the ministry she should serve in. Many envision the pastor's wife as singing and playing musical instruments, when these may not be her gifts. The wife of the minister may also be expected to hold an office in the church when she may have absolutely no desire to do so.

I believe that the minister's wife should be free to choose what's best for her and her family. By fulfilling her personal and professional goals and dreams, and serving the church in the way that best fits her talents and personality, the pastor's wife can take off the mask, and live her life fully and completely as directed by God.

Closing scripture:

"And do not be conformed to this world, but be transformed by the renewing of your mind, that you may prove what is that good, and acceptable and perfect will of God."

Romans 12:2

Chapter 11:
Defining and Embracing
Your Role

For this final chapter, we will discuss the concept of identity. The reason this book may have appealed to you, is in part because you are married to a pastor. Your role as a pastor's wife is admirable and noteworthy, but there is more to your identity than your last name and the significance of the man to whom you are married. If that title was taken away from you, who would you be? You were someone special when you were born, as you grew up and before you even met your husband. Your unique identity and personality are what attracted him to you. That uniqueness about you should not disappear once you become his wife. You are still a gifted and talented individual with your own divinely given purpose. While part of your role is now to support your husband's ministry, it is important to know what else God has ordained you to do and be.

I once met a pastor's wife named Sandra. She was married to a well-known pastor and had teenage children. She worked as a nurse three nights per week, and enjoyed her career. In previous years, she did not enjoy the role of being a pastor's wife. As a matter of fact, she hated it. She felt that she was always in her husband's shadow, and had to live up to the expectations of other people.

Over the years she learned to enjoy being a pastor's wife. She started to see his profession not as a job, but as a high calling. She started to see the people of the church, not as competitors or enemies, but as souls that needed to be nurtured. Moreover, she also started to understand her role in that process.

In her role as a nurse, she was able to care for the physical well-being of her patients, and she found that these skills equipped her with the knowledge needed to serve in the health ministry of her church.

She understood that God had brought her and her husband together as a team, to help nurture and care for the people of God. As a result, she no longer perceived her role of a pastor's wife as a chore. Rather, she began to perceive it as a privilege. She did not see it as her only purpose, but as part of the purpose for which she was called.

Sandra started reaching out more to the people at church that she did not know very well, and soon developed meaningful relationships with the families of the church.

She spent more time in personal devotion and prayer, and was able to pay less attention to how she felt, and more attention to what she ought to be doing for others. This helped her appreciate her role both as a nurse and as a pastor's wife, and helped her appreciate how she could use both roles in service to God.

Another pastor's wife by the name of Jennifer was very gifted in the area of musical talent. Jennifer played the piano and organ very well, and played for the church and for the choir. She enjoyed being able to serve the church in this way, and felt that she enhanced her husband's work by using her gifts.

Yet another pastor's wife by the name of Maria had a passion for cooking. She was also passionate about cooking healthy meals. She cooked for special occasions at the church and also delighted in cooking and hosting guests in her home. After a while, she felt the call to hold cooking classes at the church, to teach young men and women to cook. This had never been done before at her church, and the members loved it. She would plan to have cooking classes at her home and at the church, and she would invite other women to share their recipes. Before long, they were hosting potluck dinners and inviting members of the community to join them for lunch. They would feed the homeless, sick and shut-in. Needless to say; Mary truly enjoyed using her gifts in God's service.

I will share with you one of my roles that brought me tremendous blessings and fulfillment. In my work as a physician, I saw the need to get involved in the health ministry of my church. Others and I observed the rise in cancer rates among members of the community and the church. Along with others, I helped start a cancer support ministry at my local church. We would meet monthly at the church or at my home, and invited women who were affected by breast cancer to come and support each other. The group included ladies who were long term survivors of breast cancer, and some who were newly diagnosed. It was fascinating how those who had been through the experience years prior were able to encourage and support those who were newly diagnosed.

I am thankful to have had the opportunity to use my skills and knowledge to serve God's people in this way. Some of those women did not survive their illness and have since passed on. But, I will never forget the times I shared with them, and the way I was able to minister to them in their time of need. There is no greater joy than the joy of serving and uplifting the life of another human being.

As the spouses of pastors and administrators, we are given a unique opportunity to serve the people of God. It is true that the role brings with it many challenges and trials as have been addressed in this book. But if we dedicate ourselves to caring for ourselves, our families and for our church family, we will be blessed beyond measure. Serving others is the true source of happiness.

My advice to pastoral and administrative spouses is to embrace the role that God has called you to. Use your many gifts and talents in His service, and the minor inconveniences of the role will fade from view.

Closing scripture:

"For I know the plans I have for you," declares the Lord, "Plans to prosper you and not to harm you, plans to give you hope and a future."

Jeremiah 29:11

Made in the USA
Coppell, TX
24 April 2021

54460534R00069